First published in Great Britain in 2020 by Dean,
an imprint of Egmont Books UK Ltd,
2 Minster Court, 10th floor, London EC3R 7BB

www.egmontbooks.co.uk

Written by Daniel Lipscombe
Edited by Craig Jelley
Designed by Design Button
Cover Designed by John Stuckey
This book is an original creation by Egmont Books UK Ltd.

© Egmont Books UK Ltd. 2020

ISBN 978 1 4052 97264

70897/003
Printed in Italy

ONLINE SAFETY FOR YOUNGER FANS

Spending time online is great fun! Here are a few simple rules to help younger fans stay safe and keep the internet a great place to spend time.

- Never give out your real name – don't use it as your username.
- Never give out any of your personal details.
- Never tell anybody which school you go to or how old you are.
- Never tell anybody your password, except a parent or guardian.
- Be aware that you must be 13 or over to create an account on many sites. Always check the site policy and ask a parent or guardian for permission before registering.
- Always tell a parent or guardian if something is worrying you.

Stay safe online. Any website addresses listed in this book are correct at the time of going to print. However, Egmont is not responsible for content hosted by third parties. Please be aware that online content can be subject to change and websites can contain content that is unsuitable for children. We advise that all children are supervised when using the internet.

Egmont takes its responsibility to the planet and its inhabitants very seriously.
We aim to use papers from well-managed forests run by responsible suppliers.

100% UNOFFICIAL

FORTNITE
ANNUAL 2021

CONTENTS

WELCOME TO A NEW AGE OF FORTNITE!

Chapter 2 turned the world of Fortnite upside-down across the first few seasons. We've had new locations, fishing and upgrade stations - and that was just Season 1. The weapons have changed and everything we knew is different ... except for the building. We're always safe in a 1x1.

The goal is still to have fun, with as many Victory Royales as possible. You can dress however you want, dance with your friends and enemies together and we can all do it with a whole new island to explore.

Whether you're playing to hang out with your friends, compete in tournaments or complete challenges, we're with you for all the laughter. Remember, it doesn't matter if you win or lose. What's important is trying your best, learning from your mistakes and cranking out those builds!

In this annual, we're going to take a look at all the new weapons, items and locations. There will be a place to stop and do some fishing as well as some pro tactics to learn.

So, grab your pickaxe and your friends, get on board the bus and let us know ...

WHERE ARE WE DROPPING?

FLASHBACK

Before we take a look at Chapter 2 and everything that spilled out of the now famous Black Hole, we should remember Season X and the ups and downs of that time.

TIME WENT ALL WEIRD!

Season X opened with a meteor heading towards Dusty Depot AGAIN. But this time, it stopped in mid-air. With this wobble in time and space, other locations were covered in strange domes. Inside, time was thrown out the window. Each bubble held a segment of Fortnite from an old timeline!

These bubbles became known as Rift Zones. Loot Lake lost gravity and Neo Tilted became an Old West town. Retail Row was overrun by zombies and Greasy Grove came back, forcing players to dance to Taco Time!

Most importantly, a rocket was built at the depot and towards the end of the season a countdown timer pointed to lift-off.

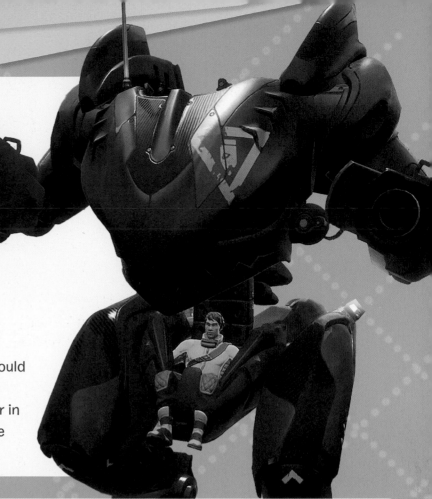

THE BRUTE CAUSED CHAOS

One of those zones brought in the BRUTE – a robot that two people could pilot and use to fire missiles. Some players loved them. Most didn't. The BRUTE was buffed, nerfed and everything in between. In the end, most people stopped using them and then they disappeared entirely.

They were seriously OP! With a huge stomp that could bring down builds and missiles that could knock a player in one hit, anyone who managed to scamper in one was likely to grab a Victory Royale. Now they're gone, do you miss them? Probably not ...

A VISITOR APPEARED

While we were all looking at BRUTEs, Rift Zones and a hanging meteor, someone had arrived at the Fortnite island. The Visitor.

Who was The Visitor? Clues point to a scientist who was examining the island and its curious environment. Players had to find tapes left behind by The Visitor during Season X. We thought they were nothing more than a bit of fun. Nobody knew the tapes warned of something big heading towards the island.

Spliced together, the tapes talked of experiments and other visitors. They told of loops and a beacon which must be activated. There were seven Visitors. There were seven rift zones. And at the end of Season X, seven rockets caused carnage on the island.

CHAPTER 2

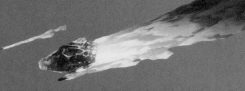

The rocket at Dusty Depot launched as the timer hit zero. The Visitor triggered something at this moment, creating a 'zero point'. As the rocket broke through the storm above the island, rifts opened across the sky. These rifts produced more rockets which bombarded the island.

Just as the chaos was calming down, a rocket broke open the vault beneath Loot Lake. Players were thrown in the air as the rockets came together. One rocket combined with the meteor as it landed to open the biggest rift so far.

Exploding into beams of pink and blue, players were pushed further into space before a whirlpool formed and sucked in the stars, space and the island itself. Everything was pulled in, reduced to a pin-prick of light.

We were left with a black hole. For forty hours we waited. Numbers appeared from the Black Hole over the first couple of hours, pointing to passages from the Visitor's tapes. And when we least expected it, Fortnite was back.

The Black Hole began to fade away, slowly revealing players walking through a new world. We got a look at the contents of the new world; the power plant, the Slurp factory and the many rivers and open spaces of water that it held.

There was fishing, boats and small glimpses of new locations before we saw Jonesy back on the Battle Bus. Familiar faces began to dive down to the new island.

Chapter 2 had arrived and with that, we're here to look at the world's favourite Battle Royale again.

Bringing up the map only showed a huge grey space covered in 'question marks'. This was our first game of a new era, and we were flooded by a host of new features, from punchcards and new weapons to a shiny new screen layout. We set out to discover the new world.

KEY FEATURES

Same name, new game. Fortnite Chapter 2 is here and it brought along lots of new ways to play. Here are some of our favourites.

FISHING

All that water brought with it lots of lovely fish. While we only started with a fishing rod, we soon got our hands on a harpoon (useful away from water too!). Catching fish became a HUGE part of Fortnite, due to the healing each fish gives. Not only that, but you can reel in ammo, materials and great weapons too! It's always worth doing a spot of fishing in your game – you never know what you'll catch.

MOTORBOATS

The Motorboat can quickly get your squad from one side of the map to the other and is packed with explosive rockets.

UPGRADE STATIONS

These allow you to trade a stack of materials to level up a weapon's rarity. Harvest mats in the early rounds and get upgrading!

SWIMMING

If you're up against a large body of water without a boat, you can build or swim. Building requires materials though, so we prefer swimming. Time your leaps out of the water right and you'll get a bonus speed boost too.

NEW LOADOUTS

As much as we loved the many weapons of Chapter 1, this new adventure stripped away a lot of choice. It made choosing your loadout much easier for a while and added a few new surprises to your arsenal.

NEW ISLAND

And of course, we can't forget a **WHOLE NEW ISLAND!** That battered old map was gulped up whole, but this new land offers so much scope for exploring, plenty of locations for events and stories. Season 2 also added a few secret HQs ...

THE MAP

A brand new Chapter means an entirely new map to explore. Let's take a peek at some of the most exciting new locations.

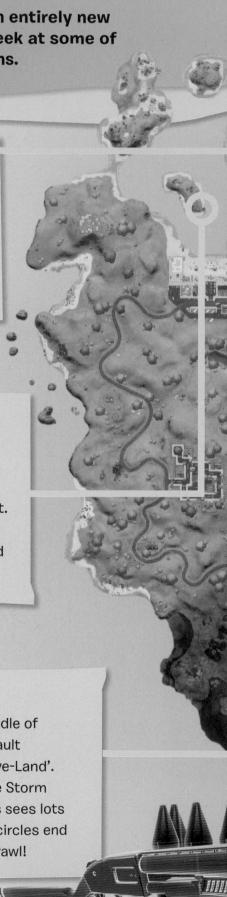

THE LIGHTHOUSE

If you want to see Fortnite at its most beautiful, you can drop far north, at The Lighthouse. There aren't many chests and you'll have to move fast if the storm says so, but it really shows off the new map.

NORTH-WEST

The North-West corner of the map holds a scattering of islands which can be tricky to navigate without a boat, but offer great cover and loot. As with the Eye-Land, if the circle ends here, it makes for an awkward fight because of all that water.

EYE-LAND

Smack bang in the middle of the island (is there a vault underneath?) is the 'Eye-Land'. Once taken over by the Storm King, this island always sees lots of activity. If the final circles end here, get ready for a brawl!

RISKY REELS

It's not Risky Reels as we knew it, but it'll do. This isn't even a named location, more of a detour from Frenzy Fields. But it's loaded with chests and metal, making it a great dropping point.

MILITARY

A great little spot away from the Docks that always houses a few chests and plenty of ammo. On top of that, the buildings and tents give out metal and wood. There are some lovely little hiding spots for some surprise eliminations too.

MOUNTAIN CAMP

You can find the highest mountains down in the southeast corner. Tucked in between the peaks is a camp with a boon of loot. The best thing about this area though, is the height. If Fortnite is all about 'high ground' then this is THE spot to aim for.

WHERE TO DROP

You might recognise a couple of the named locations as you scan the brand new map, but once again the ever-shifting sands of the island have given rise to some new named points of interest, which you can find out about below.

DIRTY DOCKS

The Docks offer so much to players who drop here. The tall cranes, of course, spill out loads of metal, but also hold chests. Head into the cargo crates to hoover up ammo and there's an upgrade station and Reboot Van if you need them. If enemies are causing you too much trouble, you can always grab a boat and get out of there!

STEAMY STACKS

To the northeast is the power plant, Steamy Stacks, a multi-layered complex with lots of twisty-turny corridors. There's a big car park if you find yourself with company, or just head towards the two chimneys where you can jump in the air and fly out of the top, to safely redeploy elsewhere.

SLURPY SWAMP

Slurpy Swamp is where all those lovely shield potions are made. There are barrels of Slurp all over the area, which can be destroyed to top-up your shield. You could jump into the vats of slurp instead, or just stand out in the river where the slurp pollutes the waters!

MISTY MEADOWS

Misty Meadows looks lovely and cosy from a distance and even up close, but when you get onto the streets, they're filled with loot and fighting. We don't mind that as it makes this new location a hotspot for some nice early eliminations and, as with most of the new areas, there's plenty of fishing holes too.

WEEPING WOODS

A river winds through the woods, but there's very little water here. What it lacks in water, it makes up for in trees, which means more wood than you can shake a stick at. There's always something new to see here as details pop up. Head for the firewatch tower to find chests and some high ground.

SWEATY SANDS

The Sands is the most dangerous holiday destination we know of. With a tall hotel, lots of small shops to explore and even a beach where you can dig up chests, it's a great place to visit. Just be careful of other players as the bountiful loot and fishing tends to attract crowds.

THE BASICS

DON'T WORRY ABOUT LOSING

You might be very lucky and score an early Victory Royale, but there's always a chance you'll lose a lot when you start out. Don't worry! Even the pro players still lose games. Just learn from your mistakes and try to improve. Losing and improving is all part of Fortnite. Focus on the fun and the rest comes after.

DROP WHEREVER YOU WANT

You'll quickly learn that some spots are more ideal for landing in than others, but they will attract the most players. Try landing in smaller areas rather than a named location and take your time to begin with. All you need to remember is to look for chests, which hold weapons and items, and harvest materials around you.

EXPLORE

Don't be afraid to look in corners, on rooftops and behind walls. Explore everywhere you want to. Doing this not only lets you know where chests and ammo can be found, but also reveals handy hiding places and escape routes.

TRY EACH MODE

There are lots of ways to play Fortnite – on your own or with friends across several different game types. On top of this, there are Limited Time Matches (LTMs), which change every week and offer unique ways to play. If you want a more forgiving mode, try Team Rumble, which pits teams of 50 against each other. If you die in this game mode, you'll respawn.

TRY OUT EACH WEAPON

There are many weapons in Fortnite and each feels a little different compared to the others. Try them all out. Shoot them at trees, enemies, or anything to see how they fire and how quickly you can reload them. Head to page 20 to read up on the different weapons in Fortnite and what their strengths are.

You might prefer to learn this aspect of Fortnite in Creative, but building is 50% of the battle in Fortnite. Learn to build the basics – it's just as important as knowing how to use the array of weapons at your disposal. Here are the basic build pieces, which can be created with wood, stone or metal.

WALL	**RAMP**	**FLOOR**	**PYRAMID**
The basic vertical cover.	Great for getting to high ground.	Good for bridges over cavernous gaps.	A useful roof that can be used as cover on top.

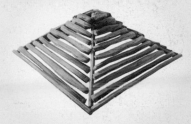

WEAPONS

Finding the weapons you like best is one of the most fun aspects of Fortnite as each one is great in different situations. A good rule is to remember that generally, the higher the rarity, the better the gun will be. For example, a gold rifle will always be better than a blue one.

KEY

☠ High Damage

⊕ Accurate

🔫⁺ Backup Weapon

◉ Close-Range

💥 Area Damage

WEAPONS

ASSAULT RIFLE

☠

Sometimes known as an 'AR', it's great for dealing damage in steady streams. It loses accuracy the longer you hold the 'fire button' but it's awesome at mid- to long-range, plus it can shred structures.

BURST ASSAULT RIFLE

☠ ⊕

More accurate than the assault rifle as it fires in shorter bursts. Not so good for taking down builds as the opponent can repair in between shots. Don't be afraid to take a few pot-shots at distant players - you'll probably land at least one hit.

SUBMACHINE GUN (SMG)

Useless at long-range unless you have an Epic or Legendary version, but even then, the SMG is most effective at close-range. Use it to blast a player or pull down their walls and floors. You might be surprised at how good the SMG is at depleting a shield. Back it up with a shotgun and it's a quick elimination.

PISTOL

The pistol can be used at longer ranges but loses accuracy. It's best used as a back-up weapon if your other guns are out of ammo. The gold version packs a punch though and can drop a player with a single headshot.

TIP

Try out both types of assault rifle to see which suits your playstyle. Test them against structures to see how quickly they can break down builds.

WEAPONS

PUMP SHOTGUN & TACTICAL SHOTGUN

The pump is slower to fire than the tactical and both are slow to reload. Which you prefer comes down to which feels better to you. As rarity increases, bullet spread and reload times shrink, countering their flaws slightly.

SNIPER RIFLE

A sniper rifle requires time and accuracy to master. It's a great weapon for a first powerful shot at a build before storming in, or it can strip a shield before you swap to an AR for the elimination.

ROCKET LAUNCHER

Rockets aren't ideal against players, though they can clutch a win. Use rockets for destroying builds or causing chaos, allowing teammates openings for better shots.

ITEMS

GRENADE

Grenades are perhaps the most helpful item for overwhelming a player hiding in their base. You can carry up to 6 of them, so spam your enemies with grenades and watch them run in fear!

TRAP

The classic spike trap was the only trap to return in Chapter 2. Nothing has changed; it can be placed on walls, floors or the ceiling. ALWAYS check before you walk into a room as a trap is often a one-hit-kill.

HEALING ITEMS

MINI SHIELD - Fills shield for 25 points (up to 50 total)

SHIELD POTION - Fills shield for 50 points

BANDAGES - Heals 25 health points (up to 75 total)

MEDKIT - Full heal

BANDAGE BAZOOKA - Holds five shots, which heal 15 points per shot. Can fill health up to 100. Once the five shots are used, it must recharge. This item takes up TWO slots in your inventory bar.

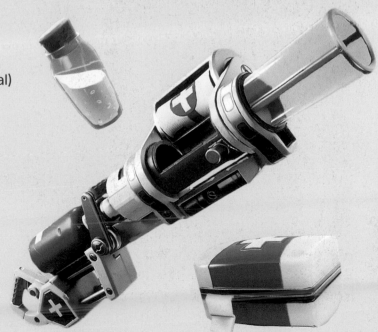

BEST SKIN COMBOS

Chapter 2 brought many changes to the game, including lots of lovely new skins to wear. We've chosen some of the best available and paired them with some pickaxes and back bling. We've also left a space at the end for you to design your own!

BIG CHUGGUS

Man and chug jug come together in this hulking skin.

JUGGUS

DOUBLE TAP

DOMINION

Hell on Earth has never looked so good.

FLAME SIGIL

BURNING AXE

PEELY BONE

Ever wondered what a banana man looks like on the inside?

SMOOTHIE

PEELY PICK

BUSHRANGER

The first skin to be voted on by the community.

BUZZY BAG

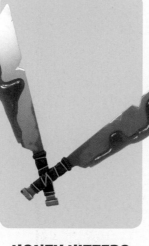

HONEY HITTERS

WILLOW

Creepy doll come to life or creepy lady who loves dolls?

DOLLY

ULTRA SCYTHE

RIPLEY

Ripley is a living, walking, shooting embodiment of Slurp Juice.

TIME KEEPER

SLUDGE HAMMER

BEST SKIN COMBOS

TEEF

We don't know what Teef is. We also don't know whether he's cute or scary.

NOSH

STICKERS

KOMPLEX

Street-smart graffiti artist with neon style.

PURPLE JAM

STREET SHINE

BUNDLES

Cuddle Team Leader got a winter makeover and looks cuter than ever!

GWINNY

POLAR POLEAXE

SORANA

This skin was a reward for a tricky challenge in Season 1.

READY RUCK

PARTY CRASHERS

CHAOS AGENT

He looks like he could invade your nightmares. He can stay in there!

OOZE CHAMBER

SPECTRAL SCYTHE

CREATE YOUR OWN!

NAME:

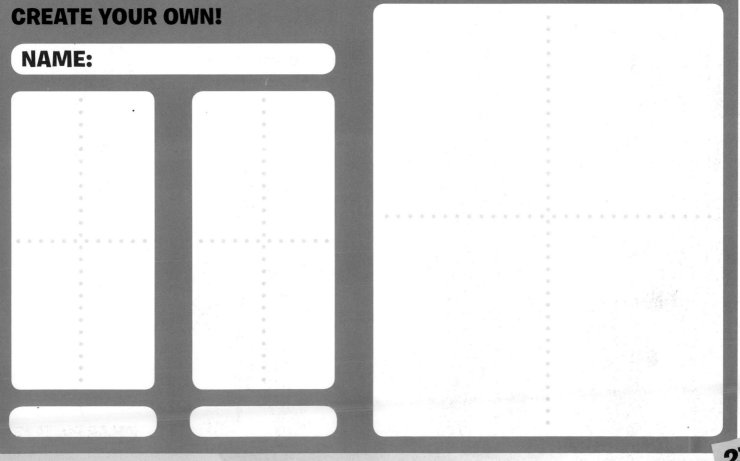

MOTORBOATS

With all that water, we needed a way to cross it quickly and what better way than by boat. Of course, this is Fortnite, so they couldn't be sailboats or canoes - we need speed and a sense of adventure! The motorboats are certainly one of the most fun vehicles we've seen for a while; they're fast, loud and full of missiles!

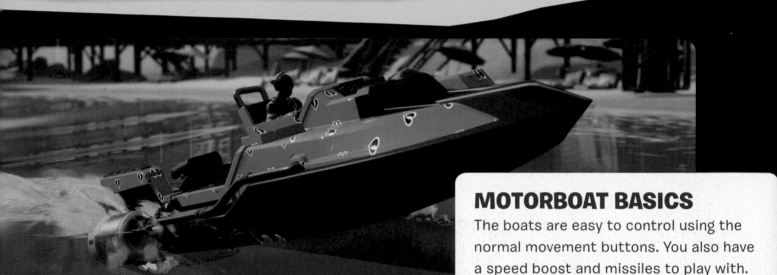

MOTORBOAT BASICS
The boats are easy to control using the normal movement buttons. You also have a speed boost and missiles to play with.

FULL SQUAD
The boat can carry a full squad of four people; however, only one person can control the boat and fire missiles.

ROCKET ATTACK
The missiles are not only great for hitting random players and other boats – if you sit a little way away from a build battle, you can fire off shots into the building to destroy sections.

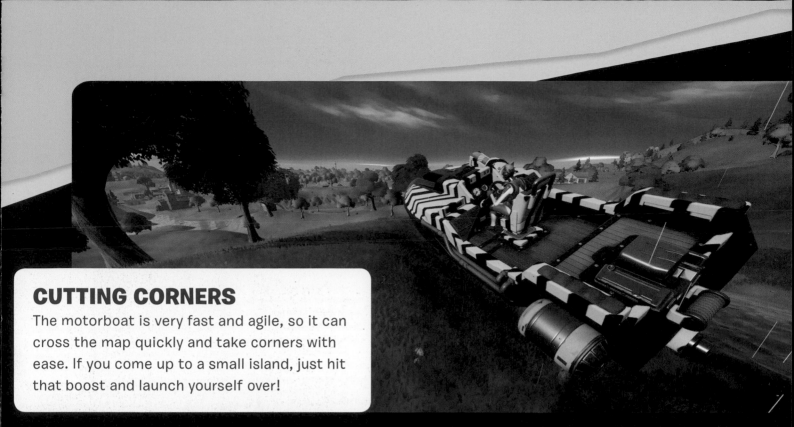

CUTTING CORNERS

The motorboat is very fast and agile, so it can cross the map quickly and take corners with ease. If you come up to a small island, just hit that boost and launch yourself over!

LAND CRUISER

You can use a motorboat on land too, although it's obviously not as effective. Boosts will push the boat along but slow quickly. If you aim a missile behind, it will explode, pushing you forward.

ZIG-ZAGGING

Make sure you don't just drive in a straight line! The boat has no roof and eagle-eyed snipers will be able to shoot you easily.

FISHING

Fishing isn't the first thing to come to mind when talking about Fortnite, but it has won over the community. It's easy, fun and it rewards players with lots of goodies! It can be done from the land or a boat and can help your match in a number of ways.

HOW TO FISH

You can fish with a fishing rod or harpoon. The harpoon is fired like a weapon and will instantly reel in your catch, but it only has ten uses before breaking.

With a fishing rod, holding the fire button will show an arc where the line will land. Once the line is cast, you need to wait. If you get a bite, hit the fire button again to reel it in.

Fishing can be done in any area of water, but if you want a good item you'll need to look for hotspots, which are white circles of moving water. Aim your harpoon or rod into this to be sure to catch something of value.

TIP

Keep moving when your line is in the water! If you just sit at the coast waiting, you'll be sniped easily.

You can catch practically everything from the water. Anything from a worthless tin can to legendary weapons and lots of fish in between. As with everything in Fortnite, it's completely random, so don't set your heart on a weapon.

TIP

You can fish through windows, so if you feel you're in danger, build a 1x1 and edit in a window to fish from.

These are the unique fish that you can reel in. They all have different uses, though they're mostly used for healing. Fish are unique because they take only a second to use, compared to the longer times of shield potions and medkits.

SMALL FRY

Heals for 25 points, up to 75.

FLOPPER

A Flopper will heal you for 50 points of health, up to 100.

SLURPFISH

This fish will fill either your health or shield, depending on which you need. It can also split its healing between the two features.

MYTHIC GOLDFISH

Cannot be eaten. When thrown at a player, it will instantly kill them and can be used more than once. However, they are incredibly rare. Only a few have ever been caught.

CREATIVE MODE

Creative mode was brought in to showcase the imagination of the Fortnite community. Before we look at how to use Creative, here are just a handful of modes that have been made possible by players, with codes to enter so you can try them out!

CODE - 6069-9263-9110

PROP HUNT

Prop Hunt is perhaps the most popular of games made in Creative. So much so that an exclusive game was launched at the 2019 Fortnite World Cup!

DEATHRACING

Deathracing also starred at the World Cup, within the Creative Cup. Deathraces are high-skill obstacle courses in which players use items and the environment to reach the finish line.

SHOTTY ONLY

This mode limits you to shotguns only!

CODE - 2991-7634-7977

CODE - 2201-4498-7425

NON-DEATHRACING

A less deadly form of racing is also possible. You can use vehicles or items like Ice Shoes.

CODE - 1330-3984-1519

CODE - 7668-2260-8816

PRACTICE BATTLE

Many members of the Fortnite community jump into Creative just to practise their skills, whether it's building or trying out new weapons.

GAUNTLET

Outrun snipers as they take the high ground and aim at racers. Your only goal is to survive!

CODE - 7352-4203-8482

CREATE YOUR OWN

With all these tools in your hands, why not create something of your own? It's hard to know exactly where to start, but all you really need is imagination and time. There is a lot to learn and plenty of pre-built items to insert into your worlds. It can still feel a little overwhelming though so here are some tips to get started.

GET INTO CREATIVE

Select Creative from the very first menu. You'll be taken to your own lobby with small portals scattered around. This is where you can input codes to try community maps or enter your own space in order to create something special.

FLYING AROUND

If you double-tap the jump button, you'll be able to fly around your build. You'll want to look at every angle of it to make sure it looks good, as well as ensuring it works as intended.

THE AR PHONE

The most important tool in your inventory. It's key to creating anything in Creative. You can use it to select items, rotate and flip them, delete placed sections and much more.

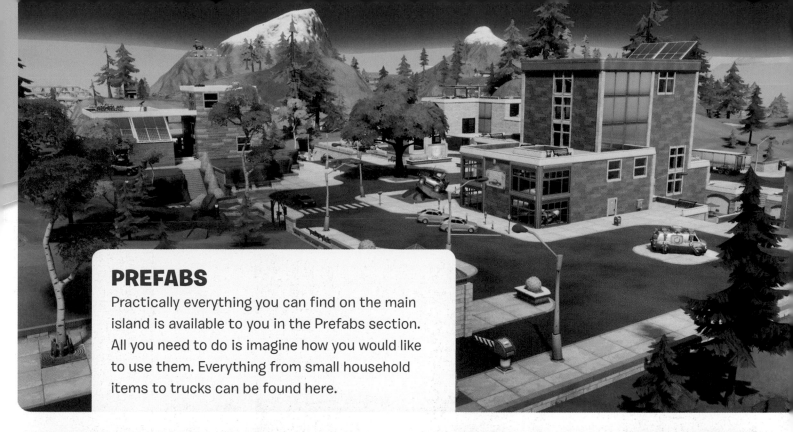

PREFABS

Practically everything you can find on the main island is available to you in the Prefabs section. All you need to do is imagine how you would like to use them. Everything from small household items to trucks can be found here.

In Prefabs, you'll also find lots of handy items, depending on what you're building. There are turrets and traps, which are great for Zone War maps and if you move into the weapon and consumables tab, you'll be able to spawn in any weapon or item available in the game.

Just pop down a building from the menu, then pull out your AR phone to tweak individual items in the building. There are HUNDREDS of items, so spend some time exploring, placing them and playing with what you have. You can always delete them if they don't work out.

SETTINGS

Within the menu you will find a section called 'My Island' and it's here that you can set rules for what you have created. Timers can be applied, spawn locations set up, and you can set the number of players, which goes up to sixteen. As with everything else, what you choose here will depend on what type of game you're building.

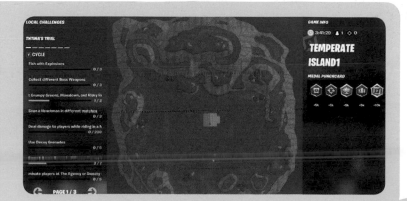

BEST OF CREATIVE

Members of the community from all over the world are creating fun minigames and most players aren't even aware they exist. Creative mode is fast becoming one of the most popular modes in Fortnite. In fact, one of the most popular reasons to play in Creative is to experience Fortnite without weapons. Here's a few different genres you'll find and some codes to try out the shining examples.

MAZES AND ESCAPE ROOMS

Who doesn't love being stuck in a room?

Escape rooms are the 'big thing' in team-building exercises, but they can be played alone too ... in Fortnite at least. These maps will test your logic and problem solving while keeping you entertained.

PROGRAM ERROR

CODE - 6939-3749-8074

In order to escape this black-and-white nightmare, you'll need to think and move fast. Program Error is a surreal maze combined with an obstacle course. Can you navigate your way out of this stylish adventure?

SLIDES AND DOORS

Ten levels of great escape rooms full of danger and excitement. Each level here is brilliantly designed and will test not only your skills, but your patience too.

CODE - 4195-4472-7967

CURSE OF THE CUBE

This creepy horror map is more than an escape room as it has large, open adventure sections. You'll want to escape from the monsters and the world around as you try to stay alive!

CODE - 3818-3420-2714

PROP HUNT

Hide-and-seek but with ... objects?

Prop Hunting was popular way before Fortnite and it was only a matter of time before we saw this type of hide-and-seek game drop into the Battle Royale. These are some of the most interesting and original takes on the classic minigame.

PROP HUNT

The most basic idea of Prop Hunt can be found in this small-town setting. Players must disguise themselves as an object and avoid being found by the seeking player.

CODE - 7376-0341-4655

CODE - 9312-2909-8471

HALLOWEEN STORY

Not much changes in the actual gameplay between Prop Hunts – there's always some hiders and a seeking team. But here, things get a little bit spookier than most hunts ... it's no wonder everyone's hiding!

PROP ESCAPE

Why not combine the objective of an escape room with a prop hunt, where everything is larger than life and a little bit ridiculous? This prop hunt welcomes the crazier aspects of Fortnite with arms wide-open.

CODE - 1885-7566-1133

BEST OF CREATIVE

DEATHRACE

One false move and it's all over!

Deathracing is a fancy name for parkour, which is a fancy name for free-running, which is a fancy name for running and jumping through a level. The odds are always stacked against you and a deathrace can go from simple and fun, to maddeningly difficult. Try to stay alive as you race through obstacles to the finish line.

FUN RUN

Fun Run aims to ease you into deathracing slowly, with some obstacles that feel much easier than others. See how quickly you can finish the course and challenge your friends to a sprint!

CODE - 0066-4697-7029

CODE - 6187-2078-9416

THE BEANSTALK

Usually deathrace courses challenge you across the horizontal plane, but The Beanstalk, based on classic fairy tales, only goes up. Watch your step, if you fall to the floor, you're going to have to start all over again!

CODE - 2037-5169-6525

ACTIVATOR RUN

Okay, here we go, it's time to step it up. Seven runners who need to reach the finish line, one player to activate traps. This is a different spin on deathracing and we apologise in advance for the frustration it will cause.

PRACTICE

We all need to practise our skills. Even the best players in the world will take time out to run through the basics of Fortnite. While you can hop into your own Creative world to hone those skills, these maps are open to all and perfect for skirmishes with your squadmates.

CODE - 1356-9797-8051

ZONE WARS

Zone Wars is the best way to practise both your building skills and weapon tactics. Play against a friend in this winter wonderland setting, which utilises presents and snowmen for a bit of a Christmassy twist.

SUPER_MEGA_VILLAIN

Why not try to break into a villain's lair? Using all the skills you'll transfer over to the Battle Royale setting; this sprawling world plays like an action film and you're the star!

CODE - 9645-2235-1747

GUNFIGHT: AZTEC TEMPLE

A gunfight can take place anywhere - why not spice it up with this Aztec setting. Available for 1v1 and 2v2, Gunfight forces you to try new things and experiment with weapons. Great for sharpening your weaker weapon skills.

CODE - 1862-5665-3754

CREATIVE BLUEPRINTS

In order to properly get to grips with Creative, let's look at building a simple idea from planning to reality. There are millions of possibilities, so let's just start with one - a simple obstacle course.

PEN AND PAPER

With all that technology in your hands it can be easy to get a little confused or find yourself overwhelmed with options. Start with a pen and paper, write your idea at the top of the page and draw out your obstacle course. Label the elements with items and prefabs you want to use. For example, note where you'll place ramps to jump from.

START SMALL

Only place a few items at a time. Don't build the whole course right away – it's likely you'll need to move pieces around. Try placing something like a bridge (it doesn't even have to be over a gap at this stage) with a couple of cars on it. Naturally players will want to cross the bridge, but this is where you'll put in some deadly spike traps to confuse players and make them think twice.

USE PREFAB BUILDS

All those pre-made buildings and structures are there to make your life a bit easier. Use them to your advantage. Even if you only use them to fill out your world, in order to create a fuller appearance. For our obstacle course, we'll just add them into the nearby area to give the course some life. We've chosen farming and industrial buildings to start with.

TRY AND TRY AGAIN

You MUST try out the course yourself. Take a step back and look at whether you can make jumps harder or easier. Perhaps you'll notice that you're bumping into a piece of scenery or an item. A player who knows nothing about your map and has never played before will need to understand everything in it. Pretend you're that player, try to react how they would and see if there are errors in your build that you need to correct before you release.

TRY TO BREAK THINGS

Test every way of navigating your level, even the ways it's not meant to be navigated, or that make it easier than you'd like. This is important so that you can create a fun level without the possibility of players finding a cheat route through. You can quickly change any problematic bits.

USE WHAT YOU'VE LEARNED

Looking at what you've learned so far and the tools you have in your hands, try to create a course. Start the course with a ramp up, maybe some ice traps to make the players movement feel wobbly, place bounce pads so that players can jump further than ever before and don't be afraid to surround them with spike traps.

CREATIVE PRACTICE

Creative mode is the best place to practise your skills without fear of elimination. Of course each Creative area is only a small slice of the world, but it's an ideal place for practice exercises. As we've seen, you can always create your own, but we've included a few drills that the pros can often be seen playing ahead of competitive matches.

BUILD OFF!

Grab a friend and jump into your own little Creative area. Once here, place a metal 'V' on the ground made from two ramps. Both players must start with shotguns and the idea is to eliminate your friend by outbuilding them to get in an advantageous position and take them out. Once somebody is eliminated, just knock the structures down and start again.

GETAWAY

Playing Getaway is very similar to the Build Off!, but for this mode neither of you are allowed to build above two layers in height. This urges each of you to use tunnelling tactics and different cover ideas to prevent elimination. Using explosives here is great fun and will see each of you panicking as everything falls down around you!

CRANKING

Cranking is a tactic to practise on your own. It's pretty simple but requires quick fingers. The idea is to build as high as possible, as quickly as you can. One technique is called 'cranking 90s' which is to place a floor, then a wall, then a ramp before spinning 90 degrees and doing the same again.

BOX FIGHTS

Box fighting is where many battles will end up – two players with close combat weapons inside a 1x1 trying to take each other out. This map was made by a content creator for players to practise moving through boxes by editing and destroying them, and battling with others in these boxes.

TIP

You can change up the rules as often as you like: different weapons, building materials, whether to use explosives or not.

CODE - 3080-7809-4388

BUILD OFF!

A game of Fortnite is often won or lost on building. You can be a crack-shot with a rifle, but if you can't build tactically, a win might always be out of reach. A strong builder will often have the upper hand on someone who prefers to just shoot. Learning to build better isn't easy, but there are a few simple builds that can improve you quickly.

RAMPING

Fortnite is about the high ground. It's easier to shoot an open target beneath you than aim at a tiny target high above. Ramping is the most basic tactic to get above your enemy. To do this, you need to keep placing ramps until you are at least one layer higher than your opponent. However, you can't just place a ramp on its own as it will be easily shot out from underneath you. They must be reinforced with a floor and a wall.

BEHIND YOU!

So, what do you do once you've ramped up to your enemy? You always want to appear behind them, and you can do this by either very simply dropping from your ramp into their base and eliminating them with a close shotgun blast, called a Shotgun Drop. Or, you can try to get around the back of their box to destroy their wall and eliminate them.

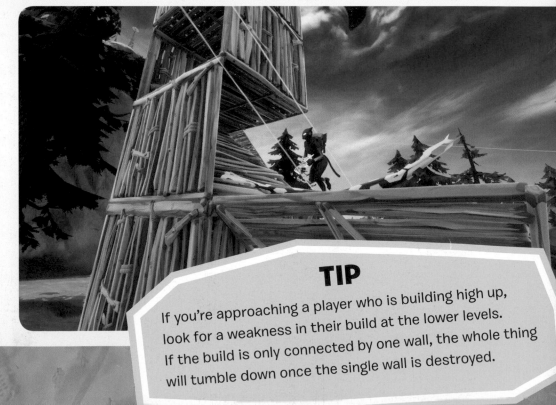

TIP

If you're approaching a player who is building high up, look for a weakness in their build at the lower levels. If the build is only connected by one wall, the whole thing will tumble down once the single wall is destroyed.

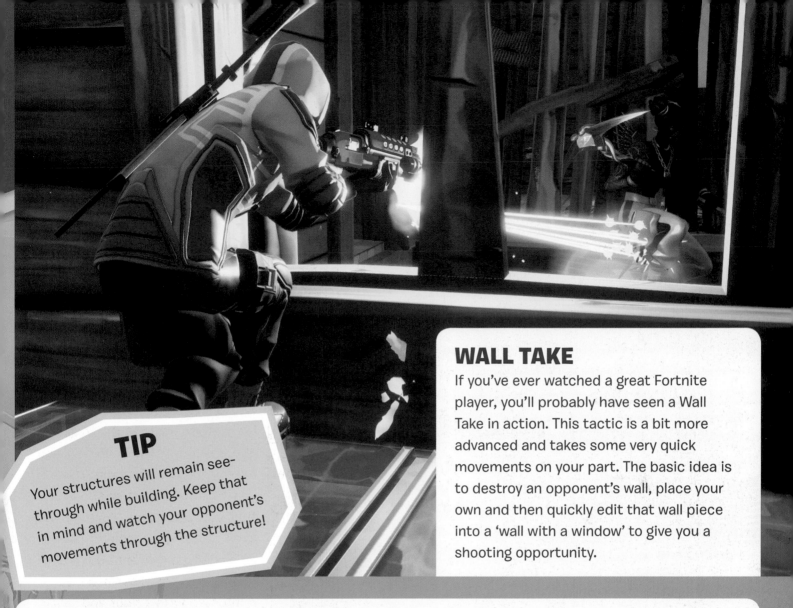

TIP

Your structures will remain see-through while building. Keep that in mind and watch your opponent's movements through the structure!

WALL TAKE

If you've ever watched a great Fortnite player, you'll probably have seen a Wall Take in action. This tactic is a bit more advanced and takes some very quick movements on your part. The basic idea is to destroy an opponent's wall, place your own and then quickly edit that wall piece into a 'wall with a window' to give you a shooting opportunity.

WATERFALLS

Another slightly more advanced technique, but this is used to escape a player or reach the ground from height safely. Waterfalling is done by falling through the air and attaching walls or ramps to the building or cliff that you're descending from to break your fall into smaller mini drops, and avoid taking fall damage.

ATTACK STRATEGIES

Attacking a player, or playing aggressively, can often result in a win if you're confident in your building and your weapons. Defending is great, but it will never secure a win, because you always need at least one elimination.

LEARN YOUR SURROUNDINGS

By exploring the map and visiting lots of locations, you can learn where it might be best to move around your opponent or get the best view for taking shots. A defending player will be on the lookout for you, but there's always a way in!

LEARN YOUR RELOAD TIMES

There's no use barrelling into an attack and mistiming the reload, leaving you open to attack yourself. Better guns reload faster, but you should always be reloading when moving.

FOCUS ON THEIR BUILD MATERIALS

If they're bunkered down in a metal base, it's going to be harder to get them. You'll need to go in with a big bang from rocket launchers or a barrage of grenades.

WORK TOGETHER

If you're playing as part of a Squad or Duo, keep talking and time your shots. One player might be best at sniping, whereas another may prefer to spray with an SMG. Try to use each other's skills as an advantage!

BAIT THE OTHER PLAYER

If you've just scored an elimination and they dropped some good loot, you can always leave it laying there. This will attract other players and you can catch them off-guard as they're collecting the goodies.

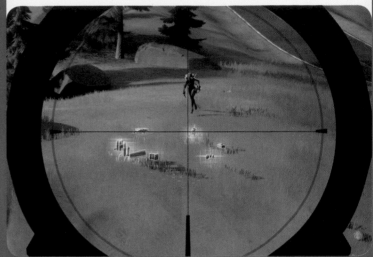

PRESSURE

If you've got an SMG or a decent assault rifle, focus your shots on enemy walls and fire constantly. Not only will they have to keep building and repairing, which uses their materials, you can look for a gap and take them out.

GRENADES!

There's no harm in spamming grenades towards an enemy! If you have high-ground and they've left an open roof or ramp, land them all inside for massive damage. This is called pocket-spamming.

HARPOONS

If your enemy is placing wooden walls or is standing on a wooden floor, just fire the harpoon at it to instantly expose them before switching to your gun.

DEFENSIVE STRATEGY

While attacking is the best way to win a game, there will always be times when you need to bunker down and defend from opponents or use tactics to avoid being eliminated. Always weigh up your best options before making the decision.

KNOW YOUR MATERIALS

Learn how long it takes to destroy each material and know when to switch. Metal is always your best bet, so make sure to harvest plenty in the early stages of a game.

WOOD
150 HIT POINTS

BRICK
300 HIT POINTS

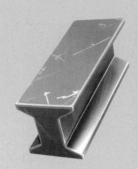

METAL
500 HIT POINTS

HEALING

While out harvesting and looting, make sure you have plenty of healing items, especially minis or slurpfish. These are the fastest way to replace your shield if you're taking hits.

PYRAMIDS

If you're healing up, even in a metal 1x1, place down a metal pyramid and sit beneath it. This provides the most cover possible while you fill your health or shields. You'll often have around 15-20 seconds of cover.

CUNNING EDITS

Enemies will take down any box you're hiding in, but they might not expect you to hide behind small edits. See if you can tuck in behind a half-wall or crouch under a diagonal to lose your tail.

TUNNELLING

Sometimes you just won't be able to get the high ground and need to stay low. Tunnelling is the best way to do this - it entails placing walls and floors as you go. Rotating your right thumbstick or mouse while placing builds will create the tunnel and protect all sides.

USE THE STORM

If the storm is closing in, keep it to your back. This will prevent players sneaking up on you, especially in the later phases as the storm does so much damage to them.

LISTEN ...

... or use the on-screen prompts if you struggle with hearing. Try to play with headphones if you're relying on sounds. The noise of approaching footsteps or someone harvesting is usually the best way to find enemies that are around you.

TRAPS

Traps are your friend. They can trigger on you and an enemy and only your foe will take damage. If you're feeling confident, lure them in and surround them with spikes!

MAJOR MOVES

Moving from point A to point B often involves sprinting across open space. But running in the open is the quickest way to get eliminated and thrown back to the lobby. There are a few techniques you can use to make sure you're not such an easy target on your travels.

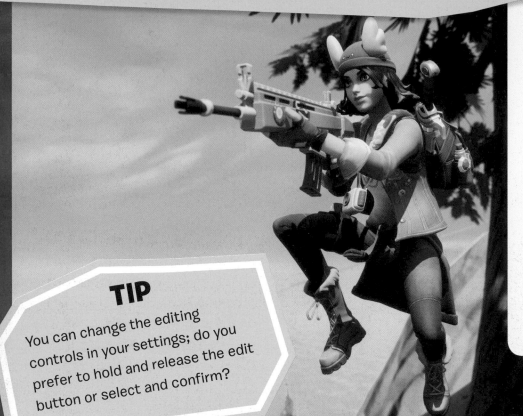

TIP

You can change the editing controls in your settings; do you prefer to hold and release the edit button or select and confirm?

NO STRAIGHT LINES

The simplest way to avoid elimination while moving is to be unpredictable. This means jumping occasionally to move your head and body out of the way of shots, plus weaving left and right as you run. Combine the two and you will make for a very hard target. The same goes for ducking often; if you do need to stop to look around you or revive a teammate, start ducking up and down. Move that head!

RUNNING WITH WALLS

If you find yourself in the open with an enemy firing at you, put walls between you by flicking your view to the sides and placing a barrier between you and the shooter. Wood will do the job just fine and you won't need to place many, just make sure you're blocking their line of sight.

RAMPS

Ramps allow you to gain elevation and provide cover. This is great for taking the odd shot at whoever has you pinned down. Use ramps so they can't see you and walk up and down them to peek out and take potshots – if they don't know where you will appear, they can't shoot you!

FLATS AND PYRAMIDS

Combining a flat floor with a pyramid on top is an effective form of cover whether you're running underneath or across the top of them. Whatever the situation, the combined pair will provide a lot of cover between you and your opponent. Running across the pyramids also moves your character up and down, making you trickier to hit.

DIAGONALS OR DOORS

Sometimes you will find yourself surrounded by structures, especially in more competitive games. Making sure that the walls around you were placed by either yourself or a teammate, you can use quick edits to pass through them and escape. With practice, it takes very little time to quickly edit a door or cut the wall diagonally in half to run forwards and make a break for it.

51

TEAM OR SOLO?

You can play Fortnite in Solo, Duo or Squad modes and you'll find that there are different strategies that work for each one. Playing alone requires you to be a master of all skills, while players in a team can cover each other's weaknesses. Here are some tips for playing alone or with friends.

SOLO TIPS

FIND YOUR DROP

Try and stick to one of a few locations to drop into; find the places you like the most. The more you stick to one place, the easier those opening moments will be because you're familiar with the area, you'll know where chests spawn and you can move through the area with ease picking up weapons and ammo.

ALWAYS WATCH THE STORM

Playing solo, nobody can help watch the direction of the storm. You need to be checking your map to see not only where the safe circle will move to, but also to guess where it might move next.

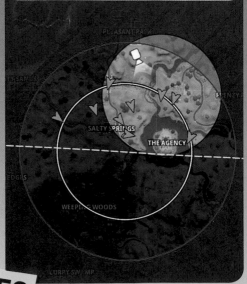

COLLECT EARLY

The opening minutes are just as important as the final few, but for a very different reason. Where the end is about high ground and fighting, the start is about laying a good base for the match. Harvest as much as possible and try to get as close to 'max mats' as you can; find the best weapons possible and upgrade them if you need to. Choosing your loadout is make or break so balance your healing and weapons the best you can.

PLAY TO STRENGTHS

If you're playing with friends, work out the strengths of everyone in the group. If one friend is a crack-shot sniper, then they need to hang back a little with a good sniper rifle. If another can find gaps in builds, maybe leave the rockets for them. These are the basics of working together - learn your own strengths and use others to cover your weak points.

WHO IS HOLDING WHAT?

With a limited inventory, there's only so much you can carry. But if there are four of you, then you can share the items across the squad. Who carries minis? Who has space for a bandage bazooka? Keep in mind, the decisions don't need to be the same every game, just be aware of who is carrying what, so when the match gets crazy, you can move towards them for help.

COMMUNICATE

Let your team know when you're moving, use the Ping system to highlight items or enemies and ask for ammo or healing when you need it. Above all, make sure you're all having fun and encourage each other.

53

SEASONAL EVENTS

Fortnite always loves to celebrate big moments from the 'real world', whether it's the release of a new film or welcoming in Christmas. The developers do their best to bring that excitement to the world of the Battle Royale. In-game events are becoming a common reason to grab your friends and revisit the island.

HALLOWEEN

Ever heard of the Storm King? As Halloween rolled in through the mist, decorations began popping up across the island. Houses had pumpkins on the doorsteps; inflatable witches stood in gardens. With no warning, the Eye-land was flattened, the houses gone. In their place stood large purple crystals and swarms of zombies big and small.

This was the calm before the storm. Soon, an LTM launched, in which 20 players teamed up to fight a giant monster who grew from the centre of the island. Eliminating him was difficult – he could heal with crystals and shoot fire blasts at players. But it wasn't all one-sided - players could harvest weapons from crystals and gain shields by killing zombies. The fight took AGES! Weak spots had to be targeted before destroying the King's horns. When he was finally downed, victors were awarded the storm umbrella for their trouble and a feeling of pride for saving the world.

CHRISTMAS

Is there an event bigger than Christmas? There certainly isn't one that gets us more excited. At the end of the year, players fighting at Dirty Docks found cargo containers filled with wooden reindeers and holly wreaths. Christmas was coming and a HUGE update covered the southeast of the island under snow.

Massive ice castles appeared within the mountains; ice cubes could be found laying around with great weapons or slurpfish nestled inside. Players could wield snowball launchers to freeze enemies, or take a more defensive approach and hide in snowman camouflage. You could also destroy the snowman disguise to garner snowballs, which you could throw at others!

And it didn't end there! Chests could now give out lumps of coal, which damaged players for 25 hit points. Wandering players could easily stumble over a gift-wrapped present too. Throwing this item at the ground spawned a present three times the size of the players and there was always a legendary weapon contained within. It really was Christmas!

ARENA

Arena is a 'ranked' game mode within Fortnite, one which tries to separate the casual players from those of higher skill levels. Arena games tend to be a lot harder and focus more on the endgame, rather than battles in the early rounds. This way of playing Fortnite can be a little hard to decipher, but we'll help cut through the confusion.

LEAGUES

Arena is broken down into three different leagues of play; Open, Contender and Champion. These leagues are then broken down into 10 divisions split between the 3 leagues. In order to rise up through the divisions and leagues, a player must increase their hype.

 OPEN LEAGUE is for friendly competition, players who love to play but strive to win.

 CONTENDER LEAGUE is much more competitive and will feature highly skilled players.

 CHAMPION LEAGUE is where you'll find players who feature in the professional tournaments such as the World Cup.

HYPE

 When you enter the Arena menu, you'll notice the flame icon. This is your hype, which acts as a points system in this competitive mode. The more hype you earn, the higher you will climb through the divisions. Below you will find the hype brackets for each division.

 OPEN I
(0 TO 499)

 CONTENDER I
(2,000 TO 2,999)

 CHAMPION I
(6,500 TO 9,999)

 OPEN II
(500 TO 999)

 CONTENDER II
(3,000 TO 4,499)

 CHAMPION II
(10,000 TO 13,999)

 OPEN III
(1,000 TO 1,499)

 CONTENDER III
(4,500 TO 6,499)

 CHAMPION III
(14,000+)

 OPEN IV
(1,500 TO 1,999)

BUS FARE

Bus fare is the amount of hype you will need to pay in order to play in an Arena match. In the first two divisions of the Open League, you won't have to pay any bus fare. From Open 3, as you leap from the Battle Bus, your hype will deplete your fare. Starting at 10 hype and increasing to 80 hype for Champion 3.

ENDGAME

It's a good idea to watch some Arena matches online because they play very differently to the standard Battle Royales. The average match of Fortnite will see only 10-15 players left as the smaller circles appear, but in an Arena match, it's more likely to be 40-50 and play continues until the circle is only slightly bigger than a player!

WHY ARENA?

Arena is where players rank up in order to be included in tournaments across the world. To be allowed to enter you will need to meet the requirements, which is usually a particular League or Division. You can find these details in the tournament menu.

DUOS TOURNAMENT
THIS EVENT STARTS IN

ESC BACK

Reach Champion League in Arena mode to unlock this event. This season of FNCS will be split into two separate tracks. All PC Duos will compete against one another in one track, while all Console and Mobile Duos will compete against one another within the other track. This tournament occurs across three rounds - Round One (Opens), Round Two (Top 1000 Duos per region) and Round Three (Top 50 Duos per region). The top 20 Duos from Round Three in each region will advance to the Season Finals at the end of Chapter 2 - Season 2. Teams will also accumulate Series Points based on each week's final placements tracked on the Series Leaderboard. Every week counts, as

SCORING

Victory Royale	+3	Reach Top 10
Reach Top 5	+2	Reach Top 15
		Each Elimination

WANNA BE A PRO?

It's entirely possible to be a high-level player and want to move your playing from casual matches with friends, to competing with the best in the world. It's not an easy road to travel – becoming a professional player requires not only skill, but patience, discipline and a positive attitude. It's a tricky path to walk, so we've plotted out some helpful tips for those who want to make the jump.

STYLE

Solo? Duo? Squad? All of them? Find where you play best. Perhaps you're great in a squad, but not so much as a solo player. When starting out, pick one and focus on that, you can expand as time goes on. If you're choosing Duo or Squads, then stick with the same players so you can work on teamwork and team chemistry.

TOURNAMENTS

Start with the online tournaments offered in-game. You'll find them under the 'Compete' tab in the menu. Here you can enter a variety of tournaments against players on the same platform (PC, PS4, Xbox, Switch, Mobile) or cross-platform. See how you do in these and if you're skilled, the progression will be natural.

TIME

Because you'll be practising a lot, you will need time. Most pro players spend eight hours playing every day - you won't be able to play as much, but if you play consistently every day, you'll improve at a steady rate.

WORLD CUP BY NUMBERS

1
World Cup

1 million
prize for each week of heats ($)

3 days
length of the Finals in New York

40 million
total participants, including those in the heats

30 million
total prize pool ($)

13
minimum participation age

100
players in the Solo finals

50
teams in the Duo finals

50,000
dollars awarded to every finalist $

23,000
capacity of New York's Arthur Ashe stadium, where the finals were held.

MAX OUT CHALLENGES

If you're reading this book, then the chances are you've already been playing Fortnite. It's also likely you'll have grabbed the Battle Pass in order to get all those lovely rewards. Each week a list of challenges is released, giving out XP bonuses and items - some can be easy, others much harder. If you want to hit the top tier of the pass, you'll need all the help you can get.

PARTY ASSIST

If you're playing as a squad, make sure to party assist your challenges by selecting it in the menu. This way when a teammate completes an action it can further your progress. This is really helpful with challenges such as 'Open 10 ammo crates at Slurpy Swamp' or 'Score 7 shotgun eliminations'. Over time you would get these on your own, but as a team, they can be completed in one match.

TEAM RUMBLE

Team Rumble is the ideal place to properly work through your weekly challenges due to the ability to respawn when you get eliminated. This is very helpful if you're halfway through a challenge and end up on the wrong end of a fight. Team Rumble also gives players a good chance to explore aspects of the map or experiment with weapons, which is harder to do in the normal Battle Royale. Because enemies are respawning too, you have plenty of opportunities for eliminations, headshots and so on.

TIP

Challenges are the fastest and easiest way to level-up through the Battle Pass, and many are great fun to complete too!

PUNCHCARDS

At the start of the day, you'll find an empty punchcard on the main menu. As you play, achieving certain milestones will reward you with a medal, which can be upgraded as you play better. Every medal has three levels, Bronze, Silver and Gold, earning slightly more XP with each level.

MEDAL PUNCHCARD

+8k   +8k   +16k

+8k   +8k   +8k   +8k   +16k

FIRST MATCH

The simplest medal to earn is this one, which just requires you to play a game of Battle Royale.

SCAVENGER

Earning this medal is as simple as looting chests, supply drops or Llamas. You'd do that anyway!

BATTLE

Grab this medal for eliminating foes. Choose a mode that lets you respawn to achieve this more easily.

SURVIVOR

If you're struggling to get kills, this medal is perfect. Just survive to be in the last 50 to get the bronze.

SNIPER

For those players with a keen eye and steady aim. You need to hit a long-distance shot of at least 100 metres.

FISHING

Take some time out from battles to land any catch with a fishing rod to earn this medal.

As you can see above, for each medal you earn, you'll be rewarded with XP that fills your experience bar. All the medals you earn will bag you 8k XP, except the fifth and tenth ones, which will double that amount to 16k XP! That's 96,000 experience you can grab in one day if you complete all the medal challenges.

MEDAL PUNCHCARD

GLOSSARY

Because Fortnite is such a massive game with millions of players across the world, it has developed a strange language all of its own. It can be a little confusing, especially if you're new to the game or watching it online. Across these pages we've explained some of the most popular terms.

ROTATE/ROTATION

Rotating is what a player does to either move behind an enemy or choose a new destination when the storm moves. Most pros will rotate to the edge of the circle, leaving the storm at their back.

PING

The Ping system is a great way to highlight a player, item or weapon without having to talk. This may happen if you're concentrating on a fight or long-distance snipe, for example.

CRACKED

If you're attacking a player whose shield is running out, you'll notice a smash sound. This is their shield being 'cracked' open, leaving the rest of the damage to target their health points.

LASERED

Similarly to 'cracked', when a player takes a massive amount of damage, you'll hear a sound like a laser being fired. This is lasered, letting you and others know they are close to being eliminated.

TURTLING

Turtling happens when a player is waiting out until the final storm circles instead of fighting. They will often sit in a metal base, doing nothing. Not to be confused with …

CAMPING

Camping describes the process in which a player sits in one place with a sniper rifle, taking shots without moving at all. Often these players are waiting for others to stumble on them, where they can then attack.

'W' KEY

When a player is being aggressive and constantly moving forward on you, this is called being "W keyed". The 'W' key on a PC keyboard is the button to move forward and this phrase mostly means you're pushing into battles.

ZONE

The safe circle. When you 'have zone' then it's unlikely you'll need to move for a while, so you can harvest more or prepare for the oncoming fight.

WHITE/BLUE

As you're attacking, you'll notice numbers popping out of your enemy. If the number is blue, then your shot has hit their shield. If it's white, then you're damaging their health instead.

STREAM SNIPER

This isn't really a term you will hear in a game, but if you watch streamers you might hear it. A stream sniper is someone who forces the game to place them within the game of a high-profile streamer in an attempt to eliminate them and find some internet fame.

HOT DROP

This used to be a location on the map highlighted in gold writing, meaning better loot. Since we no longer have those, Hot Dropping has changed to mean jumping from the bus as soon as possible.

FORTNITE QUIZ

Think you know everything about Fortnite? Then try and answer these 20 questions. Hop into the game if you're struggling to work some of them out.

1 How much shield does a mini give you?

2 Which new location provides power to the island?

3 Which fish causes an instant elimination when thrown?

4 How many uses does a fresh harpoon have?

5 Which is more accurate at range, the sniper rifle or the assault rifle?

6 How many of each mat do you need to upgrade a common weapon?

7 How much damage does a motorboat missile deal?

8 How many grenades can you carry in a single stack?

9 Which rarity is the highest quality?

10 Which material is strongest?

11 What tool do you use to place items in Creative mode?

12 How many coloured metal bridges are there on the island?

13 What landmark can you find in grid ref C1?

14 How many V-Bucks does an Epic skin cost?

15 How many tiers are in the Battle Pass?

16 Where can you watch a film on the island?

17 What was the total prize pool for the 2019 World Cup?

18 How many medal spaces are on the punchcard?

19 How many leagues are in Arenas?

20 Who placed the tapes leading into Chapter 2?

GOODBYE!

Well, it has been a journey. As Chapter 2 came out, we all panicked while Fortnite was sucked into a black hole. But it came back, and we've had loads of fun since then across many Seasons already. Events have come and gone, weapons appeared, and new items were introduced.

Fortnite is perhaps better than ever and it's only going to keep growing as we keep playing. The most important thing about Fortnite is not only how huge it is or how much it has changed video games, but the fun we have and the friends we play with. Even the Victory Royales are small compared to what we experience.

Winning is great – it's why we play Arena – but it's important that we try our best and learn along the way. Every time we jump from the Battle Bus the island is full of opportunities and moments we can create.

Whether you play on your own, with friends or with a view to turn pro, it's the game that brings us all together. It's Fortnite that brings fun and builds a community. You don't have to be good to love the game, just enjoy each moment.

NOW, GRAB YOUR FAVOURITE PICKAXE, PUT ON YOUR BEST SKIN, STEP ONTO THE BUS AND DON'T FORGET TO THANK THE DRIVER.